LET'S **see**

Ancient Mesopotamia

by **Cynthia Klingel and Robert B. Noyed**

Content Adviser: Michael Danti, Ph.D., Research Specialist,
Near East Section, University of Pennsylvania Museum, Philadelphia

Reading Adviser: Dr. Linda D. Labbo, Department of Reading Education,
College of Education, The University of Georgia

Let's See Library
Compass Point Books
Minneapolis, Minnesota

Compass Point Books
3109 West 50th Street, #115
Minneapolis, MN 55410

Visit Compass Point Books on the Internet at www.compasspointbooks.com or e-mail your
request to *custserv@compasspointbooks.com*

Cover: Reconstruction of the famous Ishtar Gate of Babylon

Photographs ©: Francoise de Mulder/Corbis, cover; Stock Montage, 6, 10, 12; Gianni Dagli Orti/Corbis, 8; Corbis, 14;
The Newberry Library/Stock Montage, 16; The British Museum, 18; Werner Forman/Corbis, 20.

Editors: E. Russell Primm, Emily J. Dolbear, and Pam Rosenberg
Photo Researcher: Svetlana Zhurkina
Photo Selector: Linda S. Koutris
Designer: Melissa Voda
Cartographer: XNR Productions, Inc.

Library of Congress Cataloging-in-Publication Data
Klingel, Cynthia Fitterer.
    Ancient Mesopotamia / by Cynthia Klingel and Robert B. Noyed.
        p. cm.— (Let's see library)
    Includes bibliographical references and index.
    Contents: What was Mesopotamia?—Who were the people of Mesopotamia?—What was important to the
Sumerians?—What was important to the Assyrians?—What was important to the Babylonians?—Why were the rivers
so important?—What was cuneiform?—What was their religion?—How do we remember Mesopotamia?
    ISBN 0-7565-0294-2 (hardcover)
        1. Iraq—Civilization—To 634—Juvenile literature. [1. Iraq—Civilization—To 634.] I. Noyed, Robert B. II.
Title. III. Let's see library.
    DS69.5 .K55 2002
    935—dc21   2002003038

Table of Contents

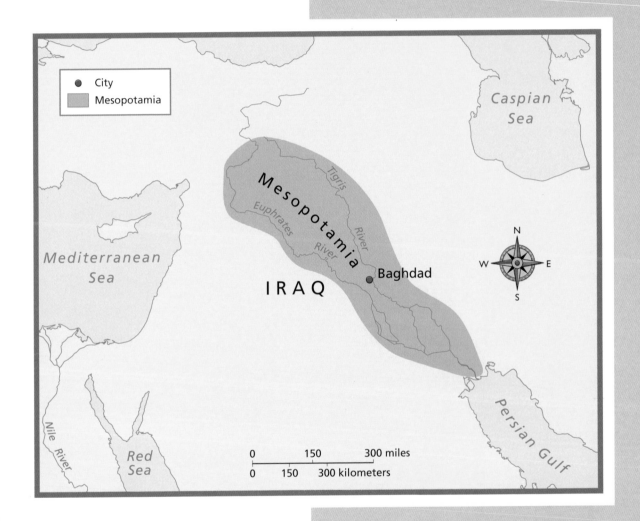

Legend:
- City
- Mesopotamia

Caspian Sea

Mesopotamia

Tigris River

Euphrates River

Baghdad

IRAQ

Mediterranean Sea

Nile River

Red Sea

Persian Gulf

N
W E
S

0   150   300 miles
0   150   300 kilometers

What Was Ancient Mesopotamia?

The word *Mesopotamia* means "between the rivers." Ancient Mesopotamia was the area between the Tigris and Euphrates Rivers. Today, that land is mostly in the country of Iraq.

The first **civilized** people on Earth lived in ancient Mesopotamia. Before that time, people traveled from place to place. They were searching for food all the time. They had no towns or laws.

The Sumerians were the first people to live in cities and make laws. The Akkadians, the Babylonians, and the Assyrians were other important groups of people in Mesopotamia.

◄ *Most of ancient Mesopotamia is in the modern-day country of Iraq.*

Why Were the Sumerians Important?

The Sumerians were settled in ancient Mesopotamia by about 3500 B.C. That was more than 5,500 years ago! They learned to plant seeds and grow food. They tamed animals to help them work in the fields. They became excellent farmers.

The Sumerians were the first people to settle in cities. Cities are larger than villages or towns. Sumerians lived in houses. They built a wall around all their buildings. Some of their neighbors were not friendly. The wall protected them from these people. Their farms were outside the walls. The Sumerians invented the first written language.

◀ *This sculpture shows Gilgamesh, a Sumerian ruler.*

Why Were the Akkadians Important?

The Akkadians settled in ancient Mesopotamia before 3000 B.C. They moved into an area north of the Sumerians. Their country was called Akkad. It was near the modern city of Baghda The Akkadians used the Sumerian alphabet write their own language.

The Akkadians were very powerful. strong armies with **bronze** weapons. A year 2350 B.C., King Sargon was their Sargon and his army conquered the S this way, the Akkadians created the **empire**. It included all of ancient

◄ *An Akkadian ruler is shown in this ancient sculpture.*

Why Were the Babylonians Important?

The Babylonian people were skilled in the arts as well as in building and farming. King Hammurabi of Babylon became very famous and powerful. While he ruled, the Babylonians controlled most of ancient Mesopotamia. He was in power from 1792 to 1750 B.C.

King Hammurabi did many things to improve life for his people. He made a number of improvements to the government. For example, he developed a set of laws for all the people of ancient Mesopotamia to follow. These laws became known as the Code of Hammurabi.

◄ *This drawing of ancient Babylon shows a tall tower called a ziggurat.*

Why Were the Assyrians Important?

The Assyrians were a group of people who lived near the Tigris River. They had a well-developed writing system. We learned most of what we know about ancient Mesopotamia from their historical records.

They became a very powerful people. They had strong armies with **iron** weapons. They rode in **chariots**. In the year 1350 B.C.—more than 3,000 years ago—the Assyrians began to invade other countries. They controlled all of ancient Mesopotamia by 900 B.C.

◄ *An Assyrian king returns from battle in a chariot in this ancient picture.*

Why Were the Rivers So Important?

Ancient Mesopotamia had two main rivers. They were the Tigris and the Euphrates Rivers. Most of the land in this part of the world was very dry. Plants could not grow there. But the land between these two rivers was green and rich. It had excellent soil for growing plants. People settled there and built towns.

Rivers were also important for travel. The people of ancient Mesopotamia could use boats to get to other parts of the land. They could buy and sell food with people from other towns.

◀ *This satellite photograph shows the Tigris and Euphrates river delta.*

What Was Cuneiform?

Cuneiform (pronounced kyoo-NEE-uh-form) was the first form of writing. Sumerians traded with other towns and other people. They needed to keep a record of these trades. They began using pointed **reeds** to make marks, or pictures, on pieces of clay. Later Sumerians used cuneiform to keep track of other important matters.

Many of the marks they made were shaped like **wedges.** The word *cuneiform* means "wedge-shaped." Not many people could write or translate this form of communication, though.

◀ *These clay tablets covered with cuneiform writing are more than 4,000 years old.*

What Was the Religion of Ancient Mesopotamia?

The people of ancient Mesopotamia believed in many gods. Four of these gods were especially important. An was the god of heaven. The goddess of the earth was Ninhursag. Enki was the god of water. Enlil was the god of air.

Each town also had its own special god. This god watched over the town. The ancient Mesopotamians believed this god owned everyone and everything in the town.

◄ *This ancient stone seal has figures of Mesopotamian gods. Enki, the god of water, is shown in the clay impression with water coming out of his shoulders.*

How Do We Remember Ancient Mesopotamia?

The people of ancient Mesopotamia started the first farms. They also created the first written language. Mesopotamians also invented the wheel. The wheel made it possible to move heavy loads. It also led to the invention of the chariot. The sailboat was another invention. Sailboats and chariots made traveling easier.

Ancient Mesopotamia is often called the "cradle of civilization." The inventions of Mesopotamia allowed people to live in cities and work together. Ancient Mesopotamia was the place where our modern way of life was born.

◄ *This early piece of Sumerian art shows a man with a four-wheeled chariot.*

Glossary

bronze—metal made of copper and tin

chariots—two-wheeled carts pulled by horses in ancient times

civilized—developed

empire—groups of people or lands controlled by one ruler

iron—a heavy gray and white metal

reeds—the tall, thin, hollow grass plants that grow in wet areas

wedges—shapes that are thin at one end and thick at the other end

Did You Know?

• Ancient Mesopotamia is also known as the "Fertile Crescent" because of its shape and because crops grow well there.

• Boats traveled down the rivers with the current. This meant they could only go in one direction!

• Some boys were chosen to be scribes. They studied twelve years to learn how to read, write, and keep records.

• Mesopotamians built tall buildings with temples on top. They thought these buildings, called ziggurats, connected them to heaven.

Want to Know More?

At the Library

Deedrick, Tami. *Mesopotamia*. Austin, Tex.: Raintree/Steck-Vaughn, 2001.
Landau, Elaine. *The Sumerians*. Brookfield, Conn.: Millbrook Press, 1997.
Moss, Carol. *Science in Ancient Mesopotamia*. Danbury, Conn.: Franklin Watts, 1999.
Service, Pamela. *Mesopotamia*. Tarrytown, N.Y.: Marshall Cavendish, 1999.

On the Web

For more information on *ancient Mesopotamia,* use FactHound
to track down Web sites related to this book.

1. Go to *www.facthound.com*
2. Type in a search word related to this book
   or this book ID: 0756502942.
3. Click on the *Fetch It* button.

Your trusty FactHound will fetch the best Web sites for you!

Through the Mail

The Oriental Institute
1155 East 58th Street
Chicago, IL 60637
773/702-9514
To write for information on the museum's collection of ancient Mesopotamian artifacts

On the Road

The Metropolitan Museum of Art
1000 Fifth Avenue at 82nd Street
New York, NY 10028-0198
212/535-7710
To see artwork from ancient Mesopotamia in the museum's gallery of Ancient and Near
Eastern Art

Index

About the Authors
Cynthia Klingel has worked as a high school English teacher and an elementary schoolteacher. She is currently the curriculum director for a Minnesota school district. Cynthia Klingel lives with her family in Mankato, Minnesota.

Robert B. Noyed started his career as a newspaper reporter. Since then, he has worked in school communications and public relations at the state and national level. Robert B. Noyed lives with his family in Brooklyn Center, Minnesota.